MW00723638

Saved, Sanctified, and Depressed

The Untreated Disease of Ministry

Dr. Preston Davis Sr.

Copyright © 2021 by Preston Davis Sr.

All rights reserved. This book or any portion thereof may not be reproduced or used in any manner whatsoever without the express written permission of the publisher except for the use of brief quotations in a book review.

Printed in the United States of America

First Printing, 2020

ISBN: 978-1-7923-5101-3

Preston and DeWanna Davis Ministries
13677 Brookview Ave.
Baton Rouge, LA 70815

mrprestondavis@gmail.com

225-329-5383

Although the author and publisher have made every effort to ensure the information in this book was correct at press time, the author and publisher do not assume and hereby disclaim any liability to any party for any loss, damage, or disruption caused by errors or omissions, whether such errors or omissions result from negligence, accident, or any other cause.

Do not disregard professional advice or therapy support because of information you read in this book. Although Preston Davis Sr. is a veteran pastor, he is providing his opinion and information, not consulting, supervision, advice or services whatsoever in this book. Unless you have entered into a consulting/supervision relationship or coaching relationship with signed forms of consent and appropriate documents in place, Preston Davis Sr is not your therapist, counselor, coach or supervisor. Nothing in this book shall be interpreted as entering you into a therapeutic, counseling, spiritual advising, legal advising, coaching or supervision relationship with Preston Davis Sr.

At A Glance

First Lady Yolanda C. Irvin

Author of The Journey

YCI Publications Kansas City, MO.

In this book, Dr. Davis' candid look into the mind of the Pastors, leaders, men, and women of God will force reality to take a seat in the forefront of your mind. No longer will you have questions to what you may have suppressed for years and refused to accept. This topic unaddressed in your life, can affect you in such a way that you will never reach the potential God has intended for you. Times are changing by the millisecond. One day you are on top of the world, basking in every luxury you can imagine, and with one tiny slip or twist of fate you have to look up to see the bottom. Are you one of those chosen few who have mastered the art "self-portrayal of excellence" to all who look upon you?

Nobody knows what to do anymore about anything. What worked before…. does not work now.

What we used to do……we can no longer do. The techniques we use to heavily rely on to get to the next level are slipping through our fingers, gone and never to return. We put our confidence in a lot of weak venues, seeking support, and no support is found. This leaves us to wear masks, hiding who we really are, fearing exposure.

Dr. Davis' cry is ……. listen to me people of God! No man is on an island. No man stands alone. We are our brother's keeper and a God released Rhema word for each brother or sister who picks up this eye-opening manuscript of transparency, knowledge, support, enrichment, and instruction.

Are you your brother's keeper? In many ways you are. When you get better, when your eyes are opened, when you deal with yourself, you can then help the next person.

Dr. Davis is not afraid to unwrap the heart of the matter of emotions most men run from.

No longer will you be blind and walk into brick walls of pain and unresolved hurt in your life.

Men of God face it! You can prepare a soul-stirring and life changing sermon, you can assist a lost sheep out of perils, spend countless hours being patient and compassionate with everyone, but never take the time to deal with you!

Now get ready to delve into the ugly, maybe painful status of your existence. You are going to soar higher than ever before. Dive deep into your need for peace and be astonished at the outcome of who you will become, after your self-examination and awakening to who you were and now who you will become.

Table of Contents

FOREWORD

Bishop Xavier D. Madison, Sr

Founder/International Presiding Prelate

Voices of Truth International Ministerial Alliance

This book offers some very sensitive, timely and thought-provoking answers to the question that so many have- how can a person be saved, sanctified, and DEPRESSED all at the same time? I believe that men and women from all walks of life who love GOD, but have silently suffered and continue to suffer the effects of traumatic experiences in places of darkness, despair, and depression, will find the way to a sense of peace and wholeness through what Dr. Preston Davis pours out from his heart via this book. Life has dealt many people unfortunate occurrences, but I believe that this book is a masterpiece which provides practical wisdom and instructions that will empower a person to be healed, restored, and meet for the master's use.

INTRODUCTION

There are many ailments that plaque the mind of the believer. We tend to have fallen into a place of uncertainty as it pertains to our faith. Regardless of denomination and or background, the structure of the church as we know it has taken a direct hit of issues of late. Growing up, going to church was expected and oftentimes ordered. We were required to attend weekly service and participate in bible studies and prayer meetings. None of which I regret. I am most thankful for the strength my mother demonstrated to guide us in the direction of righteousness.

What has taken center stage in my personal life is the concern over how many people from that era lived the life we thought were reserved for a later time. How many people dedicated themselves to serving but were never served?

It is possible, that back then the issues of today were not present some may think. I beg to defer. I believe that the issues we are experiencing today were very superbly present.

What was not present was knowledge and recognition. People had limited knowledge and hardly anyone could recognize a problem if it were not public. For example, drug abuse was something that displayed public traits. Alcoholism was a public situation even if it were kept in house. Sooner or later it showed up in the public.

Society adjusted and counted the problem as not that serious. Simply because we saw this type of behavior on the regular basis. What we did not see, we did not address at all.

Primarily because we were not prepared to treat the problem. Generations drank, nothing happened, right? Wrong. A lot happened. Think of the internal damages done to those that abused alcohol. Think of the damages done to the families involved.

We simply were not educated enough to go beyond the texts of the Sunday morning topics.

As we have witnessed, our religious leaders are now expected to go beyond the four walls of the church in addressing issues, educating the congregation, and fortifying the community.

Today's pastor must be well versed, experienced, and yet studying this thing called life.

It should not be a surprise to us that suicide, teen pregnancy, drug, and alcohol abuse, as well as designer drug use is at an all-time high. At the core of all these social issues there is yet one that has disguised itself as a shy character flaw. We are missing it from the pulpit week in and week out. People are exiting the churches by the masses now for fear and insecurity.

Men in general are walking aimlessly in their faith and some are simply walking completely away. What has been the undetected agent that has caused so many to give up, walk away, and even take their own lives? After all, they seemed so happy at church last time we saw them. They were smiling and being sociable. This is all too regular in our headlines. Same song and dance, but no answers. Being saved is great, being sanctified could never be replaced, but can one be both and depressed also? Though it sounds unheard of, and it should not be so, the answer is YES, IT IS! One can absolutely be *Saved, Sanctified, and Depressed*.

I personally believe more of us than not are conflicted between our idea of faith and the reality of life. I was taught that Christians did not experience these issues once they were saved.

I grew up believing this theory until life happened to me.

To make this simple to understand, consider this. One could be married and yet not committed. That is as simple as it gets. There are too many people going through the motion of religious participation than those experiencing spiritual wellness.

Society has become more advanced and yet less knowledgeable. We have millions of questions and maybe fifty answers. We continue to seek for the unknown while we ignore the obvious. And please do not think that I am laying total responsibility on the clergy or the church. I am saying though, that there is a great deal of responsibility being neglected in these arenas. We are overrun by doctrines of wealth and prosperity, but a broken person needs healing before they can realistically pursue anything of sustenance.

I pray that this read will enlighten you, awaken your inner being, and cause your heart to see yourself better than the state you may have been in for any duration of time.

This effort is dedicated to my mother, Mable Williams Henry, my wife, DeWanna *"Lady De"* Davis, our children, both physical and spiritual. Above all, to our God, the only True God, the one who heals.

Take this journey with us as we look to the prescription of restoration to be made whole. Completely whole, so that we will no longer have to alter your conviction of being saved, sanctified, and filled with the precious Holy Ghost!

THE PERFECT WORLD

If there was ever a such thing as the perfect world, God would absolutely be the center of all things. Looking back, groups of various interests have made it difficult in many cases to identify God. Just jog your memory a couple of decades back. We would start our days with the pledge and a prayer. I can remember the excitement I shared with my classmates at the beginning of the school day. We were always eager because we were being encouraged at home to pray. We heard grandparents and parents pray. We studied together, played together, and we worshipped together. Life was simple and innocent then. I used to hear my mother and her friends mention the good ol' days. I thought those were no such thing until someone made a big deal out of public prayer. The price of a soda went up. The ice cream or snow cone man stop coming on the regular. Then people just stop coming to church. What happened to us?

There was a time when I can recall going to the local store with nothing but a handwritten note and returning with a bag of goods. I can recall the milk man coming by and leaving milk, and juice on the stoop and nobody bothered it.

I remember going next door to borrow a cup of sugar for whatever we needed it for, and nothing was ever said. Society then, was an open care package. We loved one another, and we loved God.

Even in the hardest of time, those couples that were going through one thing or another; there would be someone who would have a little get together just to help them stay together. This was commonplace back then because people loved, and they demonstrated that love openly. When was the last time your child spent the night some place, and you were at peace in their absence?

There were no cell phones or pagers. We just went and came back. In the perfect world, children would still be playing basketball on an old dirt lot with a broken bicycle rim as a hoop with no backboard. The streetlight would still be the agent that sent you home every evening.

In the perfect world, every little boy nine years old and older, would have a bike, a gas can, and a lawn mower, managing his own business for money to buy that new pair of chucks.

We need not look too far to realize: those days are gone. That innocence is lost probably for rest of time. My heart yearns for those days my mother and her friends used to talk about the good ol' days. My children will never know the joy of playing without concern. They will never know the joy of a water balloon fight or sharing your snack with someone who did not have what you may have had. And sadly, they will never know the joy of being told stay inside or stay outside during those hot summer days at grandmother's house.

Yes, we have come an awful long way from the good ol' days. As I studied to find the root connection in the simple life and this fast-paced microwaved society, the common connector was love. A fight back then was just a reason to be better friends the next day. There was no grudge holding or no revenge matches. You fought. You either won, or you lost, but when it was over, it was over. If a kid had a gun, it looked like all the other BB guns in the neighborhood, and those were used to shoot cans and an occasional stray.

The funny thing is if I may use that terminology to explain my next point. A lot of people attend church for the wrong reason, and the most common one is attending out of habit, and not out of obligation or commitment. This happens largely in part due to the absence of a true relationship with God. We will discuss that a little later in the book.

I am not sure if we as a people really understand that we have issues both saved and unsaved. We fail to get better due to our levels of pride and education. The myth that men do not go to the doctor is more factual than myth. But that within itself is why so many men die prematurely.

And in a perfect world, we would encourage one another to seek help when something is wrong. I am convinced too that the church has a lot to do with why issues are hidden and ignored.

Remember, we live in an imperfect world. I say remember because, we need to keep that fact at the forefront of our minds. We are an imperfect people, in an imperfect world. Yet, we look for a perfect church, a perfect pastor, a perfect home, a perfect job, and a perfect spouse.

The fact that God supplied a perfect sacrifice for an imperfect people should be grounds for each of us to strive for perfection. In striving, we should want to be in better shape physically, spiritually, mentally, and emotionally.

Church as we knew it missed a lot of what we see today. The message of prosperity took us away from the earn your keep mentality. It created a culture of debt for many. I do believe we should all experience a level of prosperity but in the correct order.

How can you sell or promote something you personally do not have yourself? In a perfect world, we would be taught more, we would use the correct wording from the pulpit, and we would understand better the plan of salvation.

It is clear that most of us fly by the seat of our pants when it comes to the church setting and the expectations of God's Word. We do what we have been taught, imitate what we have seen, and never come to a true identity in our faith.

We are often time eager to serve, but do not know how to serve. We take stewardship as just a word and not a lifestyle. All these can be traced back to an earlier time when issues did not get addressed. And because those were never addressed, they have only grown worse.

In times past, as a society, have operated based primarily on what we knew. The fact that so many of our leaders were unlearned to a degree, we as followers and or parishioners were untaught. As technology evolved and knowledge became more available, we wondered into the light of the unknown. What we discovered was, certain things were either verified or ruled as folklore. We found out that, the very bible we were being taught from was oftentimes misquoted and misinterpreted.

We found out that children that displayed behavior problems actually had a condition, and the switch or belt was not the proper medication.

Most notable was the discovery of what church really represented. We even arrived at the proper criteria of selecting a leader. Unfortunately, some of the damages produced from sub-par leadership may never be corrected due to the unwillingness of some not to be enlightened, and that none of us can do anything about it.

We have primitive mindsets in a technologically advanced society, and what is staggering is the number of us that simply refuse to change.

There was a time when pastors and preachers alike, carried a certain level of respect. There was a time too, when church was a place of fellowship without regards to one's social status.

There was a time when people relied on their faith over all else. In researching for this project, I found that, when we had less, we seemed to have more. That may not register with some of you, but that is okay. I just remember when we were not so busy trying keep up with someone else. We were simply focused on getting ahead and getting better.

With all the changes we have observed in society, the only thing that seems to be locked in a vortex of stagnation is the church.

All of this brings me to the title of this work. *Saved, Sanctified, and Depressed*.

The rise of violent crimes and the scramble to live longer has never been so visible.

On any given day the walking tracks, the gyms, the weight rooms, and nutrition stores are wall to wall with people trying to better their physical health. Though there is nothing wrong with this, the health of the internal man stands neglected.

What has happened? Why are there so much unresolved issues in our lives? We are regular in church services. We attend prayer service and bible study. We treat people kind, and yet, we find ourselves empty inside.

What has become of our so-called perfect world? What has happened to the love and concern we once had for one another?

Why are our men killing one another? Why are homes being destroyed at the hands of angry men? Why are our women being abused and degraded by our men?

I am sure I could continue asking thousands of questions and connecting those to the men of our society, but that within itself would defeat the sole focus of this effort.

To our women readers, please understand this from a realistic standpoint. Our men are hurting, and the pain has been hidden for generations.

We have simply not had an avenue afforded us to treat this unspoken carcinogen in our lives.

Men have tried to walk in the footsteps of the old-time way, and we have failed to function properly because the old-time way worked for people who learned the old-time way. They worked and lived the old-time way. We live in a much different place and time today.

What was once swept under the rug, is now the focus of efforts to find a resolution.

In times past, the pastor had only a couple of things he was responsible for. Today the role of the pastor has dramatically changed, or has it? Is it possible that the role has always been what it is today? I would absolutely submit to you that the role has never changed, the expectations have.

In the past if there was an issue, the pastor had one generic answer. We will pray for you.

Though prayer is extremely important, these deep seeded issues must be addressed prayerfully and therapeutically. Where the lie that men do not cry and men do not show affection came from, I will never know. I do believe that this lie has rooted itself in the minds and hearts of our men.

Since we know that the mind is a fertile place for poison, we will prepare to address that area shortly. The bible tells us as a man thinks in his heart so is he. At least that is what we have been taught. The truth is, there is much more to that passage. Why have we only been given a portion of the meal?

As a whole, we tend to adopt anything that sounds good and eliminates our personal responsibility to anything of importance. It has been proven that we also promote the, "if it ain't broke, don't fix it", mindset. What happen to simple regular maintenance?

True: if a thing is not broken there is no need to fix it. But there is always a reason to maintenance it. Ensure that whatever it is does not break.

Can we agree that there are way too many things in our lives both poorly maintenance, and moreover, broken? It is those broken things that we should be concerned with.

When something breaks, it usually sets off a chain reaction of more items following that path even if those items are in good shape. It is only a matter of time before something from a broken section finds its way in the area of a well working part.

In simpler terms, if the mind or heart is broken, it is just a matter of time before the spirit, the will to do, the strength to pursue, and the desire to be whole is damaged.

When the Lord begin to speak to me about this project, my mind went back to some of the events of recent time involving the men and women of God that gave up on life. When we think of the leaders of the church, the heads of state, the leaders in the community, and the people responsible for educating our youth, depression seems out of place.

Is it because we think that these individuals are immune to depression? Is it because we think these individuals are made to deflect depression? Or is it because we simply have no concern for the next person?

My studies have rendered so many answers to these questions that it may be safer to just address them all. For the sake of understanding, I will give you the meat of my studies.

The minds of society have somehow become locked on, "it does not involve me". As accepted as that is today, I believe it is that thinking, that has our entire world upside down in selfishness.

What happen to our caring for the next person? We have become so independent that we could care less about anything but our own. Every Sunday morning, every single Wednesday night, parking lots fill up with impeccably dressed, hardworking people who come to hear the Word of God taught, preached, and explained. These same parking lots, with vehicles ranging from little to astronomical dollar amounts, bring with it the pains of people who come and go the exact same way, simply because they are broken when they arrive, and they depart the same way.

Pastor or teacher go home with a sense, though false, a sense that he or she has done a service of help, when in fact, nothing has been made better.

We have fallen asleep at the wheel. There are so many telltale signs that a person is fighting or battling with depression, how do we miss it? Could it be that we are too consumed with our own agendas that the programs of others are simply not our concern? Could it be that what is going on with you is none of my business, or is it we are so far from the God we say we serve, that we cannot possibly see a storm brewing?

Personally, I prescribe to the latter. Because religion has become such big business, those of us that have bought into the fly by night doctrine have evolved into a status hungry population with no desire to seek the face of the Living God.

Because we have turned away from building, maintaining, and securing a relationship with God, we have lost the compassion for one another. We simply do not care.

And the world we live in promotes this every night. The news we hear is oftentimes biased and breeds division and more isolation. Those that can afford to, move away from the troubles of just going to the corner store. Those who cannot, simply are lost in the shuffle.

What happens to the person that believes God and yet struggle every day? What happens to the person that smiles publicly and never stops crying privately? No need to wonder, they make the news at 5 and 10. They usually walk in a place of business and change the world we live in.

Yet most of these people, were good church goers. Some even taught bible study. Some of these were over our children, driving them to school, and on trips. Babysitters we hired and entrusted with our babies. Some were co-workers we have known for years.

Do I have your attention now? Look around. You could very well be sharing your office space with the very next suspect of a horrible crime.

Your pastor, your deacon, your church secretary, your youth leader, and yes, your musician could very well be a person approaching the point of no return. Have you noticed any changes in the lady you share the pew with every Sunday? Is she still talking about the goodness of the Lord? Have you noticed anything unlike her as of late?

What about the man that is always smiling and giving the youth candy and such? Have you noticed his demeanor? Is it not the way it used to be?

I have heard a lot in theory [of the signs we ignore], on why one cannot be saved, sanctified, and yet depressed. All would probably do well on a social site for discussion, but this is not that place, and I can assure you it would not do as well here.

Each week I stand and look out over our congregation and my prayer is always, God who is it?

I pray this prayer so much now that it has become second nature.

Why? I sat in a congregation broken, hurt, confused, weakened, *Saved, Sanctified, and Depressed.*

Being brought up the way most of us were, we tend to think that as Christians that everything that attacks the body is linked to our spiritual neglect. I thought the same thing! Only when I was introduced to the reality of my personal health and unaddressed items in my life, did I come to accept that my condition warranted medical attention, not an exorcism.

We could dive into the causes of a thing and define the medical terms associated with it, but that would overshadow an area outside the scope of this work.

It is to our benefit that we acknowledge sicknesses and ailments. Saved or not, you will encounter some type of ailments in the body. The focus of this work is to address the overlooked things that has caused many to give up, walk away, and in worse cases, take their own lives.

Jesus stated that He came that we might have life. I hardly think He intended for that life to be one of torment, pain, and confusion, since He did say, and have life more abundantly. Understand that this too has been taken out of context for the selfish gain of many. Life more abundantly should be understood as life in fullness. Which cannot be obtained or fully enjoyed if one is not fully well.

Today, there seems to be an influx of those trying to promote a lifestyle that is not even the lifestyle they live. We find pastors trying to embark upon mega ministries with extraordinarily little if any local support. That too, could be another book. In my research and careful observations, there are very few whole men and women of

God. If we look closely, the vast majority of those attempting to lead are in dire need to be led themselves.

Being saved is often misrepresented. We tend to think that once we are saved, we are good to go. I would like to share a personal position on this portion. I believe at the time we accept Christ as our personal Savior we then owe it to ourselves to present the whole man or woman to God for total restoration. Getting saved is like going to the emergency room. You must sign up to see the doctor. Coming into the emergency room is the first step to getting whatever brought you there addressed and treated.

Seeing that the church is our emergency room of sorts; getting saved is our first step to seeing the doctor. There is a period of sitting and anticipating what the doctor is going to find.

Seeing that we generally know already why we are not well; we need that professional to point out the treatment for our case. The problem is, we generally treat getting saved just as we do our doctor visits. We try to tell the doctor what we need and not what brought us in to the emergency room.

What happens in this case is we leave the emergency room untreated totally. The altar is the same way. We come, we accept Jesus, we walk away a new member, shake hands, and go back to our seats still broken, still untreated, and yes; still depressed.

Sadly, no one knows we are yet untreated because we are emotional. People are happy, and the issues of our heart are yet very much still in place. We return to our homes to share the news that we got saved today! Hardly do we ever hear, I was delivered today.

The backlash of not being delivered, brings us to the purpose of this writing.

An undelivered church member later becomes an undelivered Sunday school teacher, an undelivered deacon, and sometimes, and undelivered minister who sooner or later becomes; you guessed it, an undelivered pastor.

Sure, he or she is saved, but they are undelivered, and will continue to wrestle with the issues they took to the altar the day they met Christ.

Before I continue, those of you that are too deep to truly accept this fact, you may want to take advantage of the next altar call and or prayer meeting.

People do not wake up on a given day and decide to be depressed. Depression has a root.

To make it simple, depression derives from a host of unresolved emotional events that has caused a person a degree of pain, doubt, and even low self-worth. I dare not present myself as a clinical specialist in this matter. I speak only from a delivered patient's position.

Over the last decade or so, the rate of those battling depression in the clergy has skyrocketed.

Notice, I chose to use the word battle and not struggle. We battle with issues for as long as we are seeking deliverance from those issues. We will suffer with a thing if we continue to try to fix it ourselves and never give God the platform to heal us.

I struggled with depression for years. I battled because I tried to hide my depression under the umbrella of my good personality, my level of education, my success in business, and of course, my ability to resolve issues when they arise. Strangely, I was good at helping others, yet I struggled myself. When I finally made it to my emergency situation, it was at the hands of my spiritual father, who directed me to get some help from someone outside the church! I can see faces changing over that last statement. I too was a little unsure how to digest what my bishop had said to me. After all, this is a powerful man of God, an anointed vessel, a great leader. Why no oil, why no prayer? Ladies and gentlemen believe it or not, had those words not found a place in my heart that day, I would no doubt be here to share this work.

The words, "let someone help you", echoed in my head like a scream in a canyon. I think the pride that I had used to hide my issues all those years was totally offended. My bishop was wrong, what was he talking about? Does he think I am crazy or something?

Thank God for truth. Dr. Michael L. Smith Sr. knew I was not crazy, he knew I was called to preach the gospel of Jesus Christ, and he knew I was a gift to the Kingdom. On that day, he also knew I needed someone trained to address my hidden issues, my private struggles.

In that exchange, God allowed me to learn something I shall never forget. Few pastors have a leader that know when a thing is spiritual or not. To most, everything is spiritual.

Before you draw an opinion, think on it this way. Everything we do affects our spiritual wellbeing somehow or another, but not everything you struggle with is spiritual. Yes, there are spirits. But those spirits feed off unaddressed items that hinder us spiritually because the physical man is not well.

A person that struggles with alcohol for example, knows he has a problem, but he will cover that problem with denial and excuses. Until the problem itself is met head on by someone who can point that person in the direction of a better way, he or she will never accept they have a problem. Through experience, an alcoholic can be one of the greatest proofs. Until the physical man is treated, the spiritual man will never emerge.

I lived with an alcoholic. I loved him dearly. He was one of the sweetest men I ever knew. He lived a normal life Monday through Thursday. I watched him participate in church, do the right thing as a man, but the secret struggle he had always came out on Fridays.

Depression and all other hidden struggles are the same. We know how to cover them. We learn to play the game of normal and yet remain abnormal. We function but in a dysfunctional way.

The strange thing about being a patient of any sickness is you identify another patient as if you have an extra sense. No matter how dressed up they might be, you will always be able to recognize someone like you or the someone you once were.

I see a lot of ministers who are still caught in the web of falsehood. Living their lives in secret pain due to depression.

Let us look at how depression sets in. Growing up, only a few of us experienced a two-parent home. Half of those that did, experienced domestic violence, the other half may never have had that open communication with our parents that would have allowed life to be easier to cope with.

So, we grew up watching a movie called, *"Our Life"*, that never ended like we thought it should.

We grew up with truly little guidance. We had children, and we tried marriage. Only to mimic the negligence we observed growing up. The older we became, the more embedded those exceedingly small items became. Trying to make a fresh start has only been a lie to try and forget the mess we might have made the last go around.

How can anyone of sensible comprehension think, that anything unresolved can benefit any effort of progress? Which brings us back to my personal situation.

After the initial shock of being advised to get some help, I sat down and allowed my mind the capacity to go back and locate that place in my life where the seed of depression was dropped.

As a child, I experienced the trauma of losing my biological father to what we thought at the time was a simple drowning. We later were informed that his, along with my two uncles, was a senseless hate crime over some trout lines. I came to realize my issues started there.

My mother was a young lady when this happen, with four children, me being the oldest at seven. She moved us to Houston and raised us basically alone. She did remarry when I was probably nine or so.

Though we had a man in the house, he too, struggled with alcohol and drugs. Through my therapy sessions, I learned another unaddressed truth. My absence of a strong, present male figure gave me grounds of rebellion to take over.

Anger then became my go to for everything I could not understand or accurately deal with in real time. As a youth I poured my inner fears into various activities, theater, rapping, dancing, and athletics.

Being around the right class of people in each of these arenas, I excelled and made a name for myself. The sad part in all this was I was still dealing with those unaddressed issues, but no one would ever know it until something did not go my way, or the way I thought it should go.

The older I became the more I began to see that; I was not the only young man dealing with issues that were not resolved. As I continued the sessions, things begin to come into clear view for me. Discovering the truth about myself angered me even more. Yet, I did not miss church.

No matter what happen in my life, I was at church on the regular. Still smiling still playing the role. At the age of twelve, something supernatural happened. I was called into the ministry.

As exciting as that might seem to you; looking back, even in this; my spiritual guidance was minimal. Mother played the role of spiritual guide in the place of our pastor, though he did spend some time with me. Not as much as I now know was needed at that age.

My desire to preach though was real then and more so now. No matter what I did in life, I missed my father's hand. Our mother did a fine job, but she was not daddy.

No matter how old we get, I believe we all are still little boys in our hearts towards our dads.

Fast forward about ten years. Wiser, smarter, and more aware of who God is, however, still struggling with these issues. Though I have become a student of the Word, exercising my gift in ministry, and building a heck of a reputation in athletics, these unresolved issues are beginning to manifest themselves in the worst of ways. By now, everybody knows not to make Preston mad, everyone knows I have a temper; everyone except me.

Can you imagine, discovering all this in less than two sessions? I had to accept that I truly did not know me!!! I felt so lost at this moment. I did not know myself. I did not know what made me tick of sorts until this day. I cried and again, I was angry.

Discovering what was missed or missing in my life still did not give me the strength at this time to ask for help. A lot of us, speaking to men; know there is something wrong, yet we do not reach for help. We continue to function, but we are not delivered to function.

As I kept with suggestions of the sessions, the challenge became how do I escape my past pains and move forward? What did I need to do? How could I do it, and what would people think when they found out that I was not the person they saw every week?

Here is a staggering thought............. How many leaders do you think are in the position I was in today?

How many of those public figures do you think are living the life they want us to believe they are living? Ever wonder which of those fine preachers are domestic mad men behind closed doors?

We need not frown on this thought. We have seen over the years that this is a reality. People with unresolved issues do exist. The old cliché of, "hurt people, hurt people", is more than something that is passed around as simple words.

This hurt has a dangerous characteristic in that, the hurt being distributed is never noticed until its almost too far gone. The proof of this would be the testimonies of people affected by an act of violence. First words out are, "we did not see that coming. Never thought he or she would have done this or that". Please do not allow yourself to entertain the thought of something just happening or they just snapped. My dear reader, people with unresolved issues are walking volcanoes. It is only a matter of time before they get hot enough to erupt.

Cooling a volcano at its most volatile point will not eliminate the lava that will heat up again.

This was who I was, close to the stage of erupting and a cool down happens. One day the cool down stop working. Please remember I was still in church, and before anyone suggests that the church was not in me if all this was going on, reel yourself back into the focus of this writing. Everything is not spiritual until we become totally delivered.

Here is when my entire life changes. Through the sessions and some private heart to heart discussions with my mother, I found that most of my issues were MY ISSUES.

No one was to blame for the pain I carried. No one was responsible for that deep-seated hatred I carried in my heart. Although, there were so many people to lay blame on for how I got to that point.

Realistically, I cannot in good spirit even lay blame to my mother because she did the best she could. Working multiple jobs to take care of four kids. She simply did not have time to tend to the various activities we were a part of. I could not blame my other family members because they knew nothing of my inner struggles.

I did find solace in being around certain family members during these difficult times.

My Aunt Brenda, who was more like my mom, and of course my Aunt Beatrice, who till this day was always my safe haven, though I did not get to see her as often. Without question my mother's mom, Mrs. Leila Cornish, was the entire safety net for me. I would never want to be out of her presence. I recall being in junior high school and each day at lunch I would call her.

As long as she were alive, I was alive. My struggles were such a none factor to me, with Big Mama alive. I hope you can now see where this is headed. I discovered the root of my issues. As a human being we all have a sense of security. That sense of security is often established by another human who is already secure and knows how to nurture another human into that space.

I had never got there! All those who would have been able to aide me in that quest was no longer with me. I felt alone even though I always had people around me. I was afraid, even though I often protected others. Strange how life comes at you with no respect of your readiness.

Getting back to my sessions: I completed these sessions with the knowledge that I personally never matured or understood how to process loss. I took it all personal. So much so that even the most caring critique was offensive to me. Even though I knew what was being told me was good for me, it was not coming from Big Mama, Aunt Bren or Aunt Bea.

During the time my mother begin to make her final plans, God allowed me to resolve those broken issues in my heart. I came to fully accept where I was bitter, where I was lost, where I was angry, and above all WHO all this rage was directed.

For as long as I could remember, I had carried a hurt that became bitterness, and even though I hid it at the right times, it was always there. It always bothered me. And on this particular night, my mother in her final days on this side, cleared the wagon with me. At that moment, after nearly 50 years, I felt safe for real, and at that moment I knew why I had been so insecure, afraid, angry, and bitter.

I needed my mother, and she never knew. SHE NEVER KNEW!

In that one night I heard something I had never heard in my life. In that one night I heard what would have pushed me to heights unknown. My mother said to me, "I am proud of you son, you are a good man, keep your hand in God's hand and don't let people use you. You are my child, and your heart is bigger than you are. Just like the rest of my babies, but I need you to be a man, love yourself, and treat people nice. You don't owe anybody nothing son".

My heart stopped and my eyes filled with tears and she looked at me and beckoned with those long fingers. As I made my way to her bed side, she pulled me to her lap and stroked my head and said, "mama's sorry if I was not there like you needed me to be, but I did my best; as best I knew back then Pres". I sobbed uncontrollably as she continued to stroke my head, I think my hearing was suspended for about half hour because I never heard nothing else due to the constant echo of, "I am proud of you son and Mama is sorry", ringing in my head.

During this time, I had been so angry towards my wife, and so detached from my marriage, I thought she was gone. And she had every right. I was undeserving of her. One of the last things my mother said to me was, "son you have a good wife, I love De', treat her right you hear me? Don't make me get you about my De".

When I came to myself, I looked around to see if anyone else had come into the room, but it was still just mama and me. I looked at her and said, "I love you mama". She smiled and said. "I know you do".

I never got to hear mama's voice again. She was gone before I could get back to her bedside.

I remember looking in the mirror and saying to myself, "is that all it was, is that all I needed?"

All these years, that was all? The answer was yes that was it. The one thing I needed my entire life was for my mother to make me know I was loved.

Not knowing that coming up, I looked for that validation in all the absolute wrong places. Who cared what I did? Who cared if I messed up? My mama does not love me so what the heck.

Women let me say this to you; as we men need our fathers, we also need that validation from our mothers. Our mothers are the women we most treasure growing up, and they are the model of what we look for in our spouse. Do not let a man fool you and tell you otherwise. We are not very verbal in this, but it is in us to find a woman like mama.

This thing had become so hard on me that depression set in and would not release me, and I did not have the know how to break free, until my Bishop suggested to me, get some help son.

I am grateful for my spiritual father, Dr. Michal L. Smith Sr.

Until that night nothing I did, seemed to be good enough, at least not for mama, but the truth of the matter was, mama did not have time to make time trying to keep us fed, clothed, and safe.

I carried this hurt, into the pulpit, into my marriage, and throughout my life for a simple apology. An apology I honestly did not need. I found the root, and that night, I started digging to destroy that root. The more I dug, the deeper and the further that root had gotten. After all, it had been buried for almost 50 years.

Some issues are not as easy as mine was. Some issues require extensive help. I was blessed that my therapist was equipped to evaluate my situation, and direct me in the right direction.

This process took months after mother went home to Glory. There is no quick fix to tenured negative behaviors. The fix takes time, it takes patience, and it takes persistence. It takes reminding and recalling. After the man accepted where he was, I took the man to God, and that was the icing on the cake.

Since that day, God has done a work that no medicine or therapist could ever do. Although, I believe that professionals are here to help those of us who will simply seek the help.

I would suggest to any of you who are in leadership. Search your hearts honestly, tell yourself the truth about you, and be strong enough to admit you need help. Maybe you will not need a therapist, or someone more trained to address your issues. However, if you do, and some of you just may, do not reject that truth.

Embrace your needs, accept your short comings, your mistakes, your mess ups, your destructive behaviors, and reach for that help.

Depression can be tricky, and it does not always cause a person to go lock up in a room and do destructive things. However, it is still depression.

This enemy of peace has left its mark on the lives of so many of our brothers and sisters in the ministry. It is believed that over 17 hundred ministers leave their post annually due to these unresolved, untreated issues. Could you be the next person to walk away? That is a choice. If you wish to complete the task at hand, the calling on your life, no matter what it is, you will have to be whole to do so.

There is no need of laying sick hands on another sick person.

There is nothing we can do effectively in ministry if we are not well ourselves.

COMMON GROUND

The old saying, "that at some point we all have something in common", is an absolute truth. I believe we have three basic things in common. First, we have a need for strong emotional support. Secondly, we need an unwavering faith in the one true God, and thirdly, we need a dedication to that true God. Nothing hinders those common needs like unresolved hurt.

Our inability to accept these hurts causes many of us to serve God ineffectively.

Pastors, it is past time for us to come to grips with our personal status of wholeness. Too many of us sit in the church week in and week out broken, hurt, and secretly suffering because we have yet to address our true needs. Those needs are hidden behind the false personalities we want to present to the public. But what happens when the congregation goes home? What happens when things do not go the way you think they should? What happens when you look at yourself in the mirror? Has the real you stop clawing to get out of the false cage you have allowed yourself to become trapped in?

As of late, and becoming more and more common, is the acceptance of the broken leader. The tragedy in this mindset is broken people cannot assist in mending another person that is broken.

Here is the deep-seated truth. Most of us, will travel through life unaware of our brokenness, because we have operated broken for so long, that broken is the norm! We have learned to hide, ignore, and sweep under rug our struggles. What this does is, allow us to function even though we are dysfunctional.

Yet, we stand in front of a congregation and tell them that God is a healer, a deliverer, and we the leaders are sick and still chained.

Before this work started, I was constantly asking, "what is wrong with people of God leaving the church, resigning from pastoring, walking away from families, and even attempting suicide"?

I asked and I pondered only to discover, I too had been on the brink of this very thing in my life at one point. And during that very dark and challenging time, I personally saw nothing at all wrong with functioning in the role of pastor even though I needed to be pastored myself.

I will admit, coming face to face with the pain I had so intelligently tucked away in my mind did not excuse those unresolved things to stay absent from my actions. It was in the times of frustration, that not only did the pain exist, but my actions also associated with that pain was becoming harder to suppress. It became virtually impossible to deny. With each incident, I found myself drifting further and further away from who God had created me to be and embracing who my unresolved pain was making me out to be.

I will never forget the words of my mother, "Pres you cannot help nobody if you do not first help yourself". But how could I help myself? Where would I start? How long would it take, and what are people going to think?

Me watching ministers, pastors, bishops, and laymen alike, suffer like I was suffering, pushed me to a harsh reality. If I continued to play this game of, I AM OKAY, it would not be long before the world knew I was not okay.

What was it going to take before I was on the news? What was it going to take before I lost my mind? What was it going to take before I committed a crime that would land me in a cell for the rest of my life?

Let me remind you all that this writing is not for those of you who are still like I once was. There are some of you that will find all sorts of scriptures to combat this reality and guess what? I did that too! Can I save you the trouble of trying to justify your condition? Accept that there is something that needs to be dealt with in you and deal with it.

Most of us delight in knowing that people are afraid of us, but the truth is those that are satisfied with inflicting fear on others are generally afraid of something as well, and usually that something happens to be themselves.

We will tackle a dragon and the boogie man under the bed bare handed but will run and hide from the very thing that created the boogie man, OURSELVES!

When a Pastor or leader comes to grip with having some unresolved hurt or some unaddressed pains, people who are supposed to surround him or her in love and try to help them. More times than not, it is just the opposite. We assist in destroying that person.

In my personal experiences, trying to muster up the strength to first accept that there is something wrong, is a battle. Then to bring that to the knowledge of those you think are there to support you, only to find out differently, can throw a person into a tailspin of emotions.

And this is where the real battle begins. Just consider this if you can. A person that has lived a lie for 10, maybe 20 years, projected a totally healthy persona in the face of being riddled with unresolved hurt internally to finally come out and admit a problem, changes everything about them except that they need help. Most of us have played this role, and many of us are yet playing now. Some of us have mastered the art of make believe.

Here is a sobering fact: Church folk want a perfect church, a perfect pastor, a perfect service while being imperfect themselves. We hold people hostage through the chains of the past and even present struggles instead of fighting to help liberate them through Christian love and genuine concern.

Let me be perfectly honest with you, there are only a few people that will stand with you through this process. I pray you come to honor those you truly know that love you, you will need them.

It is the unstable, unproven, uncommitted, and messy person that will show their true colors when you are in the fight of your life.

It is here you will find your truth. You will learn where you stand with those you have stood with. You come to see what you really mean to those who have filled your head with beautiful words and public adoration.

You will feel the most profound distance one could feel and could live through. This is a lonely place. The truth in this is, it is a place you created.

Whenever we continue to function in the presence of hurt, pain, disappointment, dishonesty, and even trickery, we are setting the stage for abandonment.

The reason most of us choose to simply keep living the lie is because it does not take much to do. Besides, nobody knows you are struggling but you, right? Well, that is the one that matters.

Not only does God know, but you know, and chances are, someone else knows it as well.

STARTING THE PROCESS

If you are like me, starting over can be a hard task. I have never taken any joy in starting over. You learn that this process can be frustrating and very scary. This is extremely simple to understand. You are now back at the starting line of a race you had already warmed up and stretched for. You were on the second or third turn and now you must go back and start over.

The first time you were running with and against other people. Now you are running against your issues. You are now running against the things you have been chained to, and chained by, most of your life. The danger in anything that is unresolved is that oftentimes the challenge of confronting them becomes larger than your resolve.

For most, this is when the race for peace and clarity is abandoned. This is where each person must know the plan of God concerning their life. Remember, the environment we now face is the one we have created through negligence and or lack of support.

I remember the way my grandmother would wash certain clothes, and as a child who did not have to wash clothes, I always thought grandmother was abnormal in her approach, until she explained why she did certain clothes this way. She would tell me there are certain things she did not want to come out in the wash, so she would turn those inside out when it was time to wash them! Today, I see the validity in turning clothes inside out.

And you know that is just like God when He directs us to the wash board of His love. There are some things that must come out, and there are some things He ordains to be unmoved in the wash. Strangely a thorough cleaning always starts from the inside. That is generally where all the dirt is collected.

Preparing for the wash is a simple task. Take off what needs to be cleaned.

Our approach to the process is the hinderance in absolute cleaning. An unwashed anything will soon be overrun and forever stained by the dirt it collects, and this is no different in our lives. The more dirt we allow to collect the dingier our appearance becomes. No amount of detergent will change that.

Once we have gotten to the reality of knowing a wash is needed, we are then at the place to take off what is dirty. For me, this was a dark place. Everything I had put on was filthy. I had become an expert of covering up with adding new pieces. Sound familiar? I would get another degree, another trade, jump into another venture, and change careers, piling more stuff on top of stuff that needed to be dealt with, until I had too much on, and the weight of that, sent me into a downward spiral of destruction. My own and everybody I had come in contact with.

Because I had become a master of covering my inner pains, nobody knew I was suffering. In addition to my charade of being whole, I had created a false sense of existing. People saw my achievements and never took time to see ME.

This the most common demonstrated behavior of people in general. We are praise driven and that is what causes most of us the most disappointment. We grow accustom to public recognition and push further back the real issues that drives us to achieve. This only lasts for so long and then the reality of true emptiness sets in. There is no rest in the mind because we are constantly trying to jump the next smoke screen until a high wind introduces itself and the smoke is no more effective. Notice, smoke is always a distraction from the fire. Everybody tries to avoid the smoke but never run from the fire. Just light a pile of leaves and watch what effect the smoke has on those standing around the pile.

The person that will come to terms with the inner condition they are battling, the desire to be whole can finally be accepted and a remedy can be sought.

As is any other sickness; and yes, depression is a sickness. We would rather avoid the ailment and bandage our brokenness with falsehood than to seek proper help.

When the process to heal begins, we must not seek out a home remedy. A professional will be the only option, and to be clear, your pastor cannot be your only treatment platform. Depression needs to be address by a certified trained counselor. Why not the pastor? He or she, might be a bit biased or untrained to address your battle. The last thing you need is for someone else to give you another band aid. This process will require some cutting and stitching but above all some sincere recovery.

One of the most profound moments in my life occurred about 3 years ago. I had been suppressing pain, hiding struggles, and overtaken by a very unhealthy way of thinking. Every action that was meant to help me was an offense to me. I SIMPLY DID NOT WANT ANYONE TO HELP ME!

In the midst of growing a ministry, I was told point blank, "you need to take a seat SIR".

Yes, my spiritual covering spoke these words to me, and did not blink when he said it.

The ego and false personality teamed up against these incredibly wise words and told my mind something, that had I obeyed, this book would not be in your hands today.

There is always a part of us that recognizes the truth no matter how wrong we have been. That mechanism of right and wrong never dies, we simply choose to ignore it.

Starting my process demanded me to stop what I was doing, and many of you will have to embark upon this same path, and you should without delay. At this point you must dismiss the thoughts and opinions of anyone including your own. Our will to survive will kick in and tell you that you can help yourself. That is the biggest lie you will ever hear concerning your healing.

If you or anyone could do it alone, this problem we are addressing would no longer be a problem. The fact that we are powerless, we need a power that can perform and get results, different results.

When I accepted the instruction of my bishop, I experienced a helpless feeling I never knew.

Truthfully, I was totally lost within myself. No athletic accomplishments would help now, no academic achievements would sooth my inner being. I knew I was saved; I knew I was sanctified, and I also accepted, I was depressed.

Pastor Davis was depressed, and depression was running my life. The preacher who had spoken into the lives of many was now waiting on a word for himself.

The most important thing I need you to understand, once you are here, you might not get a word. Not a supernatural one anyway.

I was so confused at this point because this was the very first time, I knew God was watching over me, but He was not speaking to me. He sent one person to quicken my mind, and another person to support me through the startup process to healing.

You will have to muster up all the courage you can to keep the course of healing.

Unfortunately, you may encounter a host of emotions in the startup. That should be expected. What emotions will totally depend on you as an individual. For me, my dominant emotion was ANGER.

I stayed upset, any little thing set me off. I later discovered why anger is always the emotion that challenges us the most. It is because you are now fighting the person that others have been fighting; YOURSELF. Trust me when I tell you, there is no one who knows you like you.

My inner being was struggling to emerge, but the agent of depression, fear, and helplessness kept the inner me chained with pride.

Rumors went to an all-time high, concerning me and the ministry. Because I was in this battle of being made whole, there was nothing I could do about the talk. In all honestly, not all of it was rumor material. I did a lot of the things that were being passed around. I sat down one afternoon, and the most humbling thing happened to me. The inner me, said something other than "help me". For the first time in a long time, the voice of reason said to me, "Preston you cannot be mad at nobody! You did that mess! Be mad at Preston!"

Me? Mad at me? How was I to do that? Accepting this fact nearly killed me, literally.

Suicide was always walking across my mind. My advantage was the prayers of my wife.

Though she took several direct hits during this time, she never stopped praying for me.

And if you are to survive this, you must have someone praying for you as well as with you.

Please be reminded, there is no quick fix for the process. The only way out of it is to go through it. Quitting cannot be an option.

SURVEYING THE DAMAGES

As is the case with any war, there will be damages due to this battle. No matter how long you have been engaged, the damages are going to always to be high and costly.

After I swallowed my pride, admitted I needed to seek real help, the little boy in me cried for the two largest security blankets I had ever known. I found myself crying for my grandmother, Leila Cornish, she was the one person that I always felt safe with. My Aunt Brenda Williams who again was my refuge and protector even though we were hundreds of miles apart.

Depression is a tricky thing. Depression will cloud your mind with a lot of doubt. You will find yourself asking questions that you know cannot be answered realistically. But each time the war would progress within, depression would flash old memories and cause anger to be more visible.

Think about it this way. We tend to reflect on happier more innocent times when we feel alone. Feeling alone can be a normal state of emotions, but it should not be. Loneliness harbors suicide. What presents itself more than anything in this phase is the question of; Why am I here?

In case you have not been paying attention. The death rate for clergymen is at an all-time high due to suicide. The general public forgets that pastors are still men and women.

After the startup has begun, your emotions will wonder and cause your heart to feel faint, but this is just the beginning.

Now you must look at what your unhealthy mindset and or ungoverned actions have done.

Imagine being in war. Bombs falling, shots being fired, people screaming for help, kids crying, smoke everywhere, and buildings burning. You get the picture? Now there is a calm, a cease fire if you will. The smoke is clearing, you are now able to see the aftermath. Bodies everywhere, wreckage, and just destruction all around. You think to yourself, "Oh My God, this is horrible!"

This is the scene most of you will see when you begin to survey the damages you may have caused over the years of neglecting to resolve these inner issues. The only exception is your carnage will look a lot like, spouses, children, relationships, friendship, and marriages.

As the younger generation likes to say, "It Just Got Real."

When I took inventory of my damages, whatever strength I thought I had, was gone. Did I do all of this? What did I do to my wife? What happened to my relationship with my children? What happen to the church I pastor? I came to the reality that no one could have survived this blast.

Thank God I was wrong! Here is where I saw God's hand. Clawing and struggling from beneath the ashes was Preston. Yes me! I was also a near causality in the war. Friendly fire had buried me in the rumble like everyone else.

I found myself sorting through the damages and every once in a while, I would run across a person or relationship in my life that was hanging on for dear life. I started digging those out, cleaning them up, giving them the proper attention, and moving them far away from the war zone.

Each thing or person I moved from the rumble, I addressed. When I came up the pile that my marriage was under, I was amazed! A pile so high that I had to climb it to start the dig. The thought of any surviving underneath all these rocks and stones nearly caused me to just leave the pile and look where other survivors might be. It was here I heard God say, "DIG"! Each rock I tossed to the side, I could hear, "DIG"! My hands, arms, and back were becoming so tired and achy, I wanted to stop, again I heard, "DIG"!

God, I caused all this mess? In my mind I had made little progress and yet the command to dig was louder. I do not recall how long I had to dig, but I do remember right before I entertained giving up, I heard a faint cry for HELP!

The more I dug the louder the voice under the rumble became. At some point, I was at an opening. I could see a hand. I reached for the hand, and the hand reached for me. We locked hands and I started pulling until an arm was more visible, a shoulder appeared, then I noticed a face. It was cut, bleeding, swollen, and hard to really recognize. When I finally was able to get closer to the face, my heart nearly stopped. It was my wife. In a faint voice she asked me, "what happened? What did you do to our marriage?"

Looking around at all the other hurt things and people, this pile was the one that broke my heart.

I could only answer my wife with, "I don't know, but I am so sorry." Without skipping a beat, she wrapped her arms around me and said, "get me out of this mess".

Looking over this scene, I knew I could not take everything and everyone out of this war zone, so I grabbed the things that I needed to complete this task of liberation, and the rest I left.

I would be dishonest if I told you leaving certain things was easy as pie. This was most difficult for me. What I had to leave was the things that allowed me to function. The things that people recognized me for; and I had to leave it.

The pages of this book could never clearly paint the time frame, but just know it was not an overnight process.

Once the process starts, you absolutely must commit to it entirely.

This is when you become so transparent with yourself that you see through you. The lies stop, the hurt gets addressed, the hidden gets revealed, and the healing process begins.

I must tell you, when I started this book, I took notice of how many clergy members were taking leaves of absence, resigning, and or just walking away. This is what the research provided. Pastor and ministers who simply take leaves of absence to clear their minds usually resign or commit another offense within six months of a leave or a sabbatical. Why? Because the leave did not address the issues, and the leave only provided an escape from the responsibility of standing in front of people. I do believe there should be an annual time of refreshing for everyone.

Get away, breath, reflect, and take a serious look within. Because I traveled so much, I could easily keep my issues in the back of my mind. Pushing issues to the rear of your agenda will always prove unwise.

Our clergy have become so conditioned to think against seeking proper aid, and that it is more acceptable to take our lives and die broken than to come out and ask for help.

When you look at your leaders, what do you see? What don't you see?

With all the responsibilities of ministry, the obligations of life, and the weight of simply being, it is easy to get trapped in the cage of depression.

When was the last time you approached your leader and simply asked him or her, how are you? You need to talk? We hardly, if ever do this. And one of the reasons clergy suffer silently, stems from the observation of what the body in the churches has done to other clergymen.

The lack of trust has been the number one go to card when it comes to clergy talking about issues within. All too many times, what is supposed to be confidential in nature becomes public information if the wrong person gets wind of it. Once a leader has been labeled, there is truly little he or she can do to change the perception of the public. The damage is done.

Here is the shocking truth. When the people who should be protecting the leader join the attempt to destroy the leader, that leader has a long road to travel.

When I spoke with members in the clergy, they all cited the lack of trust, in why they have been hesitant about confiding in anyone. People just talk too much.

So, before any normal person subjects him or herself to the scrutiny of the ill-advised and or unchurched, they walk around bottled up. Another staggering find during my research was how many common issues most of the men and women I spoke with had.

Twenty percent of those polled, were sexually assaulted as youth. Over 45% were abused physically, 20% were reared in single parent homes, and 15% were under-educated.

If you look at those numbers, that is a lot to consider. More than that is the question of where does your leader fall in those numbers? We do not know, because we take none of those things into consideration when we select a leader.

I have sat in a lot of selection procedures and I have never heard anyone on the committee ask a candidate about their mental wellness. They ask about everything except that.

Would it not be wise to know if you are getting a whole leader from the start?

We move on looks, vernacular, and stature. We look at education and accomplishments, but we never wonder about emotional or mental wellness. A never-ending cycle: and sadly, the broken leader that came from his or her last assignment, will now attempt to lead you.

There is no way we can expect better from anything broken. I always encourage people to put themselves in the shoes of a leader, and see if they would be able to handle dealing with people just like they are? You would be totally surprised at some of the responses I have heard.

As comical as it may sound, in our unresolved, broken, bitter, and pain concealing beings, none of us would take joy in dealing with anything remotely favoring who we are without Christ and the mercies of God.

Men and women in leadership have real life issues; THERE IT IS! They pay for food like you, they make mistakes like you, and they avoid the hidden issues, just like you.

What is aiding in the misrepresentation of unity is the potential embarrassment that would and should follow anyone that has lived a lie for any length of time. It took me a long time to even bring myself to the mirror after my process started. I realized in all the mayhem I did more damage to me that the things I was holding in my heart.

I realized that each bout with depression was pushing me further from the truth. The fact that there were things that happened to me in my childhood that I never told; my credibility was now a question. Why? Because I had lied before. Not against another person, but a lie is a lie. How can we believe what this person is saying since he or she lied about this or that?

Hence another battleground. Most of us cannot escape; the what will the people think syndrome.

I have learned; people are going to think what you show them. Until you show them something differently.

The challenge in that is; we have shown them so many things, and it can be difficult for anyone, even ourselves, to really know who we are. I had to come to grips with the sobering fact of not knowing Preston. And someone reading this book is connecting with that.

We lose our identity in falsehood. We trade-in who we really are, for who people want us to be.

The mimic affect is full blown in our society. Everyone is trying to be like someone else.

Let us further talk about depression. The state of being depressed is when something prolongs sadness for a duration warranted by any objective reason. In short, holding on to something painful too long. In my efforts to break the cycle of depression. I found things that I had tucked away in my heart and mind that were nearly as old as I was when I started the process! Why were they there, and why so long? The answer was simple. I never told, I never opened up, and I feared the fallout.

Guess what happened? The things that bothered me earlier in life were carried into my adulthood. By now though, my childlike innocence was gone, I had learned how to use profanity, I had learned how to hit, and I had mastered belittling a person in a confrontation.

The other thing I had learned well, was how to keep a poker face. I was hard to read. My actions, however, were not. Looking back, my actions were those of a wounded little boy looking for a place to run and lick his wounds. And many of our leaders, and many of you are walking around with unresolved issues that will take its toll on you sooner or later.

I recall my wife telling me one day how mean I was. At that point, I was in total professional denial, and it did not matter what she thought, I was me, this is Preston, get out of my face, you make me mean, and the list could go on. A common response when we are wrong. Blame it on the next person.

During a session, my counselor greeted me, and we sat down to talk. Before I could get comfortable and prepare for the session, she jumped in my face with; stop acting like you're not hurt, tell me what is the damn problem, who did it to you, name them now, tell me who did it!!! Speechless and shocked to say the least. I heard a crack in my broken being. I started crying and the list was rolled out. When I tell you, I was filled with hate, I was overrun with it. I was mad about things I really had nothing to do with. I was mad for what had happened to my parent's marriage and how all that played out. I was violently angry. Dangerously explosive. As I continued to unload my pains, I was able to see the hatred I had fed, the hatred I kept, and the hatred I protected; was who I had become. I was only nice to people when I had to be and even then, it was clear that I had something else going on.

When I snapped, nothing was off limits. This was absolutely abnormal. You may be sitting under another Preston right now. Not the Preston of today, but the Preston of old.

Everything that I did not accomplish in my early life was linked to poor choices I made due to my hidden hurt. I never even thought to consider, man you need some help!

To me it was the world that was wrong, I was good. What a hard pill to swallow. It was me the entire time. The people I had held in my heart were either dead, or living the life of no Preston, while I was walking around bothered by something, they did twenty or thirty years ago.

After the shock of the session, I went home and cried in intermittent stages. Just start crying for what I thought was for no apparent reason. I learned those crying spells were good for me. I did not want to hear it at the time, but I would cry and get mad and then a calm would come. Each time I cried, I could hear that command, "DIG", all over again.

Each pain had a face, a name, a time, and a date. Each pain had a scent, and it had a casualty. In each episode of my healing, I saw more of Preston dying than anything or anyone else. The worst thing we can do when we get here is to shut down and deny you need help.

When I could see myself from the outside looking in, my heart was broken. I had lost the little guy that God had put His hands on at 11 years old. I had lost the little boy that Mable called "Petchy". I had lost compassion for others and the concern for the needs of others, yet I was standing before people. The reality of my mental capacity at the time was critical. I wonder how long would it have been before I would have simply exploded, and changed the lives of many of people forever? We are not comfortable getting this deep, but we need to. Not everybody will seek the help I sought.

What is your leader holding on to? What are you holding on to? The reason the rate of suicide has skyrocketed in recent years has all to do with the things we have not dealt with.

We take so much for granted. Never even considering as we go to our various places of worship what mindset our leader or leaders are in. We never know, simply because we never ask.

We must accept the fact that people will hurt you. What you do not want to do is supply the ammunition they need to accomplish that task.

We need not train our eyes and attention on just the church leaders. These issues are not discriminatory. Notice how some of our celebrities have been discovered with many issues.

Actors Leading With Depression and Acute Personality Disorder.

Is it safe to consider that these individuals had these issues long before they became celebrities?

People struggle with different things, but if we simply leave those things unaddressed, the result could be devastating. When we see the news reports of mass murders and things of that sort, our minds should always wonder about the mental stability of the person that carried out such acts. Leaders in general have been allowed to function under silent duress for so long, that most of us think this is the way it is supposed to be.

Men and women of God do not allow your pain to become your prison. There is a way out.

For some of us, climbing out is possible, for some digging out, for some scaling out, but for the majority of us, we need help to get out. Let me try to clarify these methods.

GETTING OUT

As I previously stated, getting out of a dark place should be the goal of everyone.

However, some of us become accustom to the darkness and we tend to just exist there.

But to every situation there is an exit. Finding that exit is often the difficult part.

For me, trying to find the exit was painful and frustrating. I had been in this dark place so long that I had erected mirrors to make it look like a regular good place to be. Like some of you, I found myself trapped by those very mirrors. Everything was a reflection of something else. There was always more than one of me! Some of you will get that in a few moments.

Everything was doubled or tripled. I had to take drastic measures. I had to start destroying mirrors. One at a time, mirrors were being broken. One by one I destroyed a reflection of Preston. When all the mirrors were gone, I stood in the rubble of glass looking down at broken reflections of the person I had become. Just like those pieces on the floor, I was broken.

This is when self-worth is questioned. I pray that you will not get confused right here. Self-worth is not the issue, your brokenness is. What you are worth right now must be pushed to very rear of this space. What you need right here is how much you have left?

A broken person cannot yield anything less than a broken appraisal. Broken appraisals are secret agents of suicide.

When I got to this place, I realized just how far away from life I was. I quickly realized too, that I did not feel comfortable with thoughts of suicide, so that meant I had to do something to live.

I determined then, that when I leave the earth, I would leave whole, NOT BROKEN.

I ran towards the smallest shimmer of light. Light in this case is help. When you arrive to this place, what people think or say is totally mute, you just want out!

Be aware that light can be scary for one that has been without it for as long as I was.

When you seek help, the question of "who" is always paramount. Then, there is the how much question? To avoid frustration of looking at the cost of a resolution, we should ask, "how much am I worth to myself?" If you try to put a price on help based on what you have, you will relapse, and find yourself facing those mirrors again.

I had to get to the place of discovering; what was I willing to invest in my wellness. What was Preston worth to Preston? Think about it this way. Most of us, up to the breaking point have operated under the false value of others. We have operated in a false sense of reality. We have operated under hidden stress, and never considered what it was costing us. We have kept a fictional persona to please the masses, our family members, and never thought of the cost. Wellness and being set free should not be a challenge. What are you worth to yourself? How far are you willing to go FOR YOU? When I arrived at this place, my deepest hurts were revealed.

It was here that the negligence to myself kicked me in the stomach. Here I stood, broken, looking for an exit, helpless, and yet still standing. How is it possible for us to do so much for others, and neglect our own wellness? The answer takes us back to the beginning. The expectations of people, the responsibilities of positions, and the roles we play in ministry. Not one of those ever allows you to simply be you. You are either husband, pastor, daddy, spiritual father, counselor, confidant, or something other than just you. The cruel reality is that these roles, and that is what they are, never afford us the capacity to simply be ourselves. In a weird type of way, we tend to think being ourselves is not enough. The light came on right here! Why was I not enough? I could be me and occupy those other spaces. I realized that I had allowed the roles to hold me, and not me holding the roles. And you can believe me when I say people will place you in roles, and never think about you as a person, and because it is pleasing to them, we slip into these roles never to return to being ourselves. Now, not every person of the clergy becomes victim to these things, but for the most part, do. So, entangled that we become the roles and reality escapes us. We stop living and simply practice and oftentimes perfect existing. Think about it, how many leaders do you know that are simply being themselves? Most of us are trying to imitate someone else, live above our means, do what another pastor is doing, and never realize you are not them. What they do might be good, but it may not work for you the same way. Once we are in that cycle, we are doomed to meet disappointments and depression.

Getting out begins with, introducing you to you all over again. If you are honest, you too will discover, that you have alienated yourself for the benefit of acceptance.

Success in my life was never a result of me trying to be someone else. My influence in ministry was not tied to a false identity, it was portrayed by a false persona! Who you saw was not who I was. The smile was always bright it just wasn't genuine. For each person getting out of this place will defer. For me, there was a lot of clawing, digging, falling, and finally a desperate scream for help! This is no easy task. Again, you will be fighting the one person that should know you better than anyone else, You! Here is where the rubber meets the road.

I have had a many fight growing up. Been in a few battles too, but nothing in my life prepared me to face Preston. This dude was tough, and he came with weapons.

I struggled, and I wanted to give up so many times. What compelled me to press forward was the desire to experience freedom. True freedom.

Believe it or not, people say they are free all the time, and when I hear that, I wonder to myself, "free from what?" I used to say those same words. They sounded good. True freedom for me is being released from those secret things that control your life. We miss this looking at our leaders because we see no chains or other devices of restraint. But mental, psychological, and emotional chains are not visible to the naked eye. If only we could hear what we do not see. We would be speechless at the rattling of chains as people would walk pass us. Here is a very sobering thought. During one of my sessions, my counselor said to me, "Preston has it ever crossed your mind that in your regular visit to the supermarket, that there is probably twenty-five people in the store at the same time that are on the verge of a breakdown?" Do you know how realistic that is?

Please do not think people wake up and decide to just disrupt lives, just because. There are triggers, and triggers cannot do anything without a firing pin. Life and the unaddressed items serve as bullets, the wrong word, the wrong actions at any given time serves as gunpowder in the bullets, and if the arms of life swing in the wrong direction those forces can collide, and life changes for everyone. Since my true deliverance, I look at people totally different. I see people as being potentially me before God saved me from me.

My dear reader, your pastor might be an undelivered Preston. Scary huh? The tragedy in this is, we take for granted that this is real. But look again, why are pastors, ministers, leaders, husbands, wives, and laypersons alike falling from ministry? Why are we, not more sensitive to the person we look to for guidance?

What has made us a society of people that tend to think this cannot happen to my leader?

Wake up people, your leaders are human. And considering this, no one ever seems to think to check on the well-being of the leader.

Because leadership can be such a strain on everyday living, those of us in these positions need a regular source of release. Getting out of this place requires another platform to direct an energy source that must go somewhere. One of the greatest mistakes for me, was trying to get more word through studying. Dissecting the books, all over again. Epic fail! Is this not the same thing that introduced me to an unhealthy me? Indeed! Yet, because we have programmed ourselves to revert to the Word of God on all fronts, we never understand that we are creating an unhealthy cycle afresh. To those of you who are sitting with your mouths open in awe, allow me to explain to you a remarkably simple principle. The reason we have become overwhelmed in the first place, is because we have failed to live. If all we do is bible study, church, prayer service, seminars, revivals, and more church, when do you live? When does your wife see her husband and not the pastor? When do the kids see dad and not the preacher? When does the neighbor talk to John, Dave, or Preston instead of the pastor? We cannot totally free ourselves of these roles if we constantly play them.

There must be a time when the pastor is off the clock. Never off the job, but off the clock.

Getting out means just that, getting out. Try being romantic again without the church as a backdrop. Try supporting a child at a game or school play without you being the star.

Try learning a new hobby to give your mind a new avenue of exploration. I had to accept that the things I enjoyed doing were all somehow connected to ministry. I love golf, but I played with other preachers! I loved sewing, but again I was always thinking about sewing something religious or inspiring. Love to cook, but this was not what I was passionate about.

With all this newfound energy and time to burn, I had to find something to do. And to my surprise, I found true freedom in the one thing I had taken for granted for several years. I learned to do NOTHING! Yes, absolutely nothing. I learned to stay home and be still. Something I had never done. Getting tied up in the ripping and running, Preston had not learned to be still.

There was always something to do, and always some place to go. Coming out of the hold of depression the most valuable tool you will find is the tool of still. Bear in mind that this is a major find. Though it has been there the entire time, we are now aware of it and its importance.

What has amazed me is the value of being free to not do anything. I have taken solace in having the freedom to relax. For most, a vacation is our time to unwind. I too thought this to be so until I went through this course of my life. I learned that vacations should be time to power up. We should unwind daily. During my vacations, my wife and I challenge each other. We do things people we know may not do. These activities serve two-fold. The first, it reenergizes the mind to venture out of the normal, and secondly, it adds a new appreciation for life and each other.

How many times have you gone on vacation only to return wishing you had more time to do something you did not do while you were there?

You did not unwind, you did not enjoy yourself, you simply went on a trip.

This is the tricky part of getting out. I like the use the life of a trucker to drive home this point. A truck driver goes down the road loaded. He or she cannot get another load until the load they are carrying is delivered or offloaded. When we go on vacation, we should unload before we leave and reload while we are gone, so that we can deliver when we return home!

A clear mind is a sharp mind, a sharp mind is a powerful mind, and a powerful mind is a healthy mind. The question to be answered now is, have you found yourself in the pages of this book? Does any of this make sense to your situation? Are you tired of being held hostage by the opinions of people? Are you worth fighting for? Do you believe you have more than enough to get free?

How many more sleepless nights are you going to have? How long do you think your smile is going to disappear? Have you decided that enough is enough?

Can I encourage you? You are worth the fight, you are worth every effort, God is counting on you, and I believe you can make it.

You have nothing to be ashamed of when you come to the truth of life. You might discover you have been in the place too long, and by all means; we need to accept that there may be some things you may not be able to recover, coming out.

RESTORING YOU

Once you are truly released and free to be you, take time to recover properly. Do not rush back into the strains of ministry. Learn to pace yourself and enjoy life. Schedule your duties and delegate what you can without impeding on your responsibilities.

Set time to simply be freed of any obligations. Develop a" NO" in your operation. You cannot accept every invite, and you need not sacrifice your life to please people.

Remember where you have come from, reflect regularly. For me this gave a new sense of redemption and mercy. Each day, you will discover the true love God has for you in the simplest of things. Cherish those things, nurture your faith, and be ever so mindful of the liberation you now experience daily.

Secure those relationships that might have been previously unimportant to you at some point in your past. Forgive yourself daily of the mistakes you may have been totally responsible for, and try to mend anything broken, if you can. The objective here is to never become bound again.

One of the many things I have employed in my daily walk is the help of someone else. Find that one person in your life you can absolutely talk to. The person that is willing to see and hear you as the person you are, and not the office you hold.

It is unfair to you to share your life with people who only see you in your office.

Each day, I tell myself, "you are God's man, you are saved, you are sanctified, but no longer depressed, stay that way", this works for me. I am so grateful to God for the very few people I have designated to be my support. These are people I totally trust. They have proven themselves trustworthy, and they play extremely vital roles in the balance of my life. What I had to accept in determining who I trusted, was they may not be trusted by anyone else. This means your choice of people you confide in might not be at the top someone else's list. Do not let that deter you from trusting them. Remember, your choices are yours, but too, your consequences will be yours as well. You must do your due diligence in securing proven allies. Anything beyond this will absolutely be detrimental to your success.

Staying free is a choice, but it is a challenge as well. You must never allow yourself to think less of yourself, your abilities, and your calling. God knew what He was doing when He chose you.

It is now up to you to be who He called you to be. As you grow in this newfound freedom, invest more each day in yourself. Be your biggest support, be your strongest alley, be your greatest fan, and above all, love yourself unconditionally.

If you will allow yourself the space to change daily, grow daily, and be better daily, the challenge of being your best will be effortless. Remember again, you are one of those who accepts that you are human. You have had your trials, and though you have been under great pressures, you did not quit! You are now ready to move forward and not look back. If you are at this place, you should be able to say without any reserve, the journey has been worth it. What you lost; you lost. What God has in store for you will outweigh the losses. As a man or woman of God in this arena of leading people, do not forget to be led. If all you do is lead, sooner or later you will find the need for leadership yourself. Secure that now. Make sure you have a good working relationship with your own leader. For some of you, you may have to go back and get some things right with your leader. You may need to clear the air, because again, you really do not know what struggles your leader may have had or is currently having. The key is to look at everyone else as if they could possibly be the old you. Just like we walked around looking healthy being unhealthy, the cycle has not stopped because we got out. My prayer is that you will share your story, your struggles, and your triumph with those you encounter. You never know what your testimony will do for the next person. Think of what it has done for you.

In closing, I think we all have need of being set free. Especially as leaders. We tend to prolong the process by worrying too much about the outcome of a thing. For me, when I stopped putting so much weight on folk, and what they would think, I was free to heal.

You have the right to choose what you allow in your life as well as who you allow. Be honest in your self-evaluation of things and make those hard decisions. You know who is good for you, and who is not. Do not be afraid to disengage. The more you deny this truth the harder becoming free will be. In the end, what you do for you will outlive what others say about you.

The power to live is in your hands, the power to sound free is in your mouth, and the power to be free is in your actions. I would much rather be free than to sound free.

Be yourself, you are so much better at that than trying to be someone else.

Today, my bout with depression is over, but the challenge is ever present. I have made it my business to never step into that ring again. Depression is a fierce foe. Undisputed for those who attempt to fight it alone. As you start the process to heal or finish the process of being free; leave depression and live in peace. Do not allow yourself to be captured again. You are worth the fight, your family is worth the fight, and above all, your ministry depends on your fight.

If you are to help heal, you must first be healed. There are just too many sick people trying to get others well. God bless you, your ministry, your efforts, and your families, I hope you can now or soon be able to declare, I am saved, sanctified, and no longer depressed.

About the Author

Dr. Preston Davis is the Senior Pastor and founder of Grace Fellowship Christian Assembly in Denham Springs, Louisiana.

A student of the Word of God and one of the hidden gems in ministry.

From the small quiet town of Stamps, Arkansas; he is the son of Clarence and Mable Davis.

Dr. Davis is an honor graduate of Bethel Seminary and Aldine High School. He is a husband, father, grandfather, author, and public speaker. Dr. Davis is the visionary of I AM M.E., an all men fellowship that allow men of all walks, to come together and share life experiences for the better good of all.

This work is dedicated, to the memory of Mable Williams Henry and the strength she gave me and my siblings to live. My siblings who are the best there is ANYWHERE. Towanda, Tony, Kim, Heather, LyShawn, Osie Jr, Steph and Dr. Krystal. My Aunt- Mom Brenda Miller, my aunt Deloris, my extended moms, Mama Norma and Judy Johnson. My dad's, Gene Henry and Henry Conley. My dear friend, Bishop Edward Brooks, thank you, and nothing else needs to be said. To Dean Tom Pitts. To my GFCA family, Deacon Henry Jackson, Minister Katina Jackson, and Tonya "Sheriff" Matthews, I love you all so much. Thank you for your prayers and support.

To our children, Carzavier, Takeshia, Karrius, Quayshaun, Kianna, Wytajah, PJ, DeAndre', Zahiria, Shaska, Ahmecca, and Quineciya, our grandchildren, and family members.

To my mentors, Dr. J.L. Davis, Uncle Votis, Aunt Gert, and all my babies in Buckner, AR.

Aunt Beatrice, Uncle Fred, Uncle Claude, and Aunt Ann. The entire Davis Klan, Madison, Shepherd, Cooper, and Washington Klan. The Brown and Gilkey family of Stamps. To the person that pushed me to start and finish this work, Lady Yolanda Irvin, thank you woman of God, your Ministry is amazing! Thank you for inspiring and guiding me through this process. To the man who changed my life while growing up, Mr. Vernon Lewis, thank you Sir. Also, to the person who taught me true sportsmanship and dedication, Kevin Mason, your friendship is a jewel. Blessings to you Mama Debbie and Granny. To Mr. Charles Calhoun who showed me what a real man looked like many years ago (R.I.P.).

Special Mention

I would like to furthermore mention some incredibly special people that have made a great impact in my life, and because of you, my life has been made better: Mr. Allus Hubbard (R.I.P.), Jewel Hubbard, Chip Hubbard, Shorty Hubbard, Edneetra Sharp, Mitch and Gary, Milton and Winfred (R.I.P.), Kevin Ener (R.I.P.), Pearly Marshall (R.I.P.), Gidget Marshall, Derrick and Marvin Gage, Chris Matthews, Bishop Lisbon Wilkins (R.I.P.), Pastor and Lady Pitre, Bridgette Martin, Pastor Tasha Dillon, Ricky Porter, Rev. Alvis Hamilton, Aunt Helen Hamilton, Coaches Jesse Cassard, Dan Hartwick, and Ralph Aldridge. Big sister, Shelia Ford, little sister, Vanessa Burse, big brothers, G. Davis, Rev. Leo and C. D. Daniels, Dr. C. Geason, and Dr. J. Coleman.

This work is especially dedicated to my father, the late James Earl Watts, my beautiful grandmother, the late Vanella Watts, my uncles, the late Clarence Bomber Watts, and Eddie Watts Sr. To my favorite clown sister, Vanella Clark, and my uncles and aunts on both sides of the Cloud-Watts clan. My great grandparents, the late Pa-Pa Fred and Mama Cuda, all my cousins, especially those special ones, Vanella Watts Smith, the late Lil Eddie, Will Cloud Jr., Big Putt, and Rev. Marvin D. Cloud. Please understand that my not mentioning your name does not devalue your significance in my life. I love and appreciate you all. Thank God for all of you.

Thank you all for taking this ride with me……….

Pres

Gone But Not Forgotten:

Mrs. Mable Williams Henry "MAMA"

To My Wife

This work would not be possible if it were not for my wife, **Pastor DeWanna "Lady De" Davis**. Thank you, my love, for everything. You have been the best thing to ever happen to me in human form. I honor you, and I am grateful to God for trusting me with you.

Made in the USA
Middletown, DE
28 November 2022

16236698R00046